ISBN 978-0-259-86633-6
PIBN 10828308

English
Français
Deutsche
Italiano
Español
Português

www.forgottenbooks.com

Mythology Photography **Fiction**
Fishing Christianity **Art** Cooking
Essays Buddhism Freemasonry
Medicine **Biology** Music **Ancient
Egypt** Evolution Carpentry Physics
Dance Geology **Mathematics** Fitness
Shakespeare **Folklore** Yoga Marketing
Confidence Immortality Biographies
Poetry **Psychology** Witchcraft
Electronics Chemistry History **Law**
Accounting **Philosophy** Anthropology
Alchemy Drama Quantum Mechanics
Atheism Sexual Health **Ancient History**
Entrepreneurship Languages Sport
Paleontology Needlework Islam
Metaphysics Investment Archaeology
Parenting Statistics Criminology
Motivational

ARTICLES OF FAITH,

AND

COVENANT,

ADOPTED

By the First Congregational Church

IN CONCORD, NEW-HAMPSHIRE,

JUNE 1, 1826.

YOU believe, that there is one true GOD, the Father, Son, and Holy Ghost: that the Scriptures of the Old and New Testament were given by Divine Inspiration, and contain the only perfect rule of faith and practice: that GOD maintains a righteous government over all creatures: that Man has fallen from the state in which he was originally created, and is by nature entirely destitute of holiness: that an Atonement for sin has been made by the Lord Jesus Christ, so that repentance and faith are now the conditions of salvation.— You believe in the necessity of our being renewed by the agency of the Holy Spirit; in the increase in holiness, and perseverance unto salvation, of all who truly believe; in the doctrine of a general resurrection, and a future judgment; in the everlasting blessedness of the righteous, and the endless punishment of all the finally impenitent.

THUS YOU BELIEVE.

COVENANT.

ACKNOWLEDGING your infinite obligations to be the Lord's, you profess your desire, in sincerity of heart, and with a deep sense of your unworthiness, to lay hold on his holy and everlasting Covenant. You give up yourself to GOD the Father, as your God, your Father, and your eternal Portion. You give up yourself to the blessed Jesus, the Redeemer and Head of the Church, as your Prophet, Priest, and King, and rely upon Him alone for salvation. You give up yourself

to the HOLY SPIRIT, and rely upon Him for sanctifica-
tion, guidance, and comfort.

Depending on Divine Grace for assistance, you here-
by solemnly bind yourself to glorify GOD, by a faithful discharge of the duties of sobriety, righteousness,
and godliness, and by a diligent observance of all his
Commandments and Ordinances——You particularly
engage to walk with this Church of CHRIST, faithfully
attending the public worship of GOD, the Sacraments
of the New Testament, the Discipline of his Kingdom,
and all his sacred Institutions, and watchfully avoiding
whatever is contrary to purity, peace, and love, as
becomes the followers of the meek and lowly JESUS.

All this you do, relying on the blood of the everlasting Covenant for the pardon of your sins, and be-
seeching the glorious GOD to prepare and strengthen
you for every good work to do His Will, working in
you that which is well pleasing in his sight, through
JESUS CHRIST, to whom be glory, dominion, and praise,
forever and ever.

THUS YOU PROMISE.

ON your thus professing and promising, we receive
you as a Member of this Church, and admit you to the
full enjoyment of all its privileges—promising, through
Divine Grace assisting us, to aid you in the duties of
the Christian life, by our prayers and fraternal watch-
fulness; expecting, in return, the same offices from
you, that the purposes of this holy Covenant may be
answered.——The LORD make us faithful to Himself
and to each other.

This Church was gathered Oct. 17, 1711.

Rev. Samuel Phillips ordained Oct. 17, 1711,
Died June 5, 1771.

Rev. Jona. French ordained Sept. 23, 1772,
Died July 28, 1809.

Rev. Justin Edwards ordained Dec. 2, 1812.

CONFESSION

OF

FAITH AND COVENANT;

Adopted by the South Church in Andover.

————

1. YOU believe in one only living and true God; the Father, Son, and Holy Ghost; and that it is the duty of all intelligent creatures, to love and obey him.

2. You believe that the bible is the Word of God; that it was given by the inspiration of the Holy Ghost; and is the sufficient and only rule of faith and practice.

3. You believe that God created man upright; you believe the fall of man, the depravity of human nature, and that men, unless they are born again, can never see the kingdom of God.

4. You believe in the incarnation, obedience, suffering, and death of Christ; his resurrection, and ascension; that he alone, by his suffering and death, hath made atonement for sin; and that he ever liveth to make intercession for us,

1*

5. You believe that Christ hath appointed two special ordinances, viz. Baptism and the Lord's Supper; that baptism is to be administered to unbaptized adults, who profess their faith in Christ, and to the infant children of members of the church.

6. You believe the future existence of the soul; that there will be a resurrection of both the righteous and the wicked—a day of final judgment; that all will receive according to their works; that the wicked will go away into everlasting punishment, and the righteous into life eternal.

COVENANT.

You now, humbly and penitently asking the forgiveness of all your sins, through the blood of the great Redeemer, give up yourself to God, in an everlasting covenant, in our Lord Jesus Christ; and as in the presence of God, angels, and men, you solemnly promise, that by the assistance of the Holy Spirit, you will forsake the vanities of this present evil world, and approve yourself a true disciple of Jesus Christ, in all good carriage, toward God, and toward man.

`And you likewise promise, so long as God shall continue you among us, to walk in communion with the church of Christ in this place ; to watch over other professing Christians among us ; to submit to the power and discipline of Christ in his church, and duly to attend the seals and the censures, or whatever ordinance Christ has commanded to be observed by his people, so far as the Lord, by his word and spirit has, or shall, reveal to you to be your duty ; adorning the doctrine of God our Saviour in all things, and avoiding the appearance of evil ; and by daily prayer to Almighty God in the name of his Son Jesus Christ, you will seek for grace to keep this covenant.

ANSWER

Of the Rev. Samuel Phillips to the question—What shall we do, that we may keep in mind our Covenant ?

1. VERY diligently and devoutly attend to the Covenant, whensoever it is publicly propounded to any person ; and yield your assent and consent to every article and tittle of it.

2. Not only wait upon Christ at his table, on all opportunities; but always eye the Lord's Supper as the SEAL of the Covenant. And every time you partake, realize that you have bound yourselves afresh to keep Covenant with God; for, to take the Sacrament, is to take the oath of obedience and loyalty.

3. Look upon the Holy Scriptures, in your daily reading of them, as the book of the Covenant; for so it is, inasmuch as it exhibiteth our duty towards God and man; and also, what we may hope and expect to receive from the hand of God, if we keep his statutes. Exod. xxiv. 7.

4. Labour to have it impressed and fixed upon your minds, that heaven and earth are witnesses of your covenanting with the great God; and that God, angels, and men, will certainly appear as such, either for or against you, in the day of reckoning.

5. Discourse frequently together of the things pertaining to the kingdom of God; and particularly of the covenant; viz. the precepts, prohibitions, promises and threatnings; of the vows, which you have made, and the comfortable experience, which you and others have had of God's gracious presence, &c. This practice

as also to quicken unto obedience.

6. Frequently renew your Covenant with the Lord in secret, as becomes those who resolve to stand to what they have said;—this is not only the duty, but (I should think) will be also very much the delight, of a sincere soul; and a choice help it is to revive our remembrance of the Covenant, and to excite our affections; and to quicken us to mend our pace.

7. Keep your Covenant by you, as a memorial of the solemn transactions which have passed between God and you, and frequently review the same.

8. And lastly, prayer must be always one direction. And this duty must be attended and performed, not only in public, and in and with the families, which you respectively belong unto, but also in secret;——*Thou, when thou prayest, enter into thy closet, and when thou hast shut thy door, pray to thy Father, which is, in secret.* Matt. vi. 6. This duty of secret prayer I hope you do not dare to neglect; you cannot (I think) ordinarily omit it, if you have a living, holy principle within you;—well; and you must pray especially for

spiritual blessings ; and in particular, that the Lord would please to put his law in your inward parts, and write it in your hearts ; " that He would make it ready and familiar to you, at hand when you have occasion to use it, as that which is written in the heart;—that He would work in you a strong disposition to obedience, and an exact conformity of thought and affection to the rules of the divine law, as that of the copy to the original." You have a disposition this way already;—pray that it may abide and grow, and plead that precious promise in Jer. xxxi. 33.; and, the more you are disposed this way, the less danger will there be of your forgetting the Covenant of the Lord your God.

USE.—From what has been said, let professors be exhorted to put one another in mind of their Covenant duties and obligations. It is true, we may not watch over others, and neglect ourselves, as some (to their great reproach) are said to do.; neither may our charity end at home ; for the law of God obligeth us to love our neighbour as ourselves. And again it is written, Exhort one another daily.—And it is remarked concerning those that feared the Lord, that *they spake often one to another*; Mal. iii. 16.—and have we not expressly bound ourselves, by Covenant, to watch over one another? Yes, verily : How then shall we dare to neglect it; especially considering that a great deal of sin and sorrow might (probably) be prevented, if professors would in this way be kind and faithful to one another? Thus, for instance : when a neighbour or brother is observed to be going into temptation, or in present danger of falling into some transgression, it is not improbable that these words, spoken (in a suitable manner) in his hearing, *remember your Covenant*, would prevent his fall ; or, if he has already fallen, it may be those words—would be the means of recovering him out of the snare of the devil ; and of bringing him unto unfeigned repentance.—And so ; if you see a brother, backward to any good work, respecting either God or man ; perhaps this memento—would shame and quicken him. Now, we are undoubtedly obliged to do this, and much more, to prevent each other's hurt, and to promote each other's good ; O ! let us not be negligent.

CATALOGUE

———◆———

Wid. Sarah Abbot

Wid. Phebe Abbot

John Abbot

Dea. Isaac Abbot

Wid. Sarah Abbot

Caleb & Deborah Abbot

Mary Abbot

Wid. Hannah Abbot

John L. & Phebe Abbot

Moses & Elizabeth Abbot

Enoch & Nancy Abbot

Wid. Abigail Allen

Wid. Elizabeth Abbot

Ezra & Hannah Abbot

Benjamin & Mary Abbot

Nathan & Hannah Abbot

Priscilla, wife of David
    Abbot

Eunice, w. of Prince Ames

Elizabeth Abbot

Hannah Abbot

Rhoda Abbot

Anna Abbot

Wid. Mary Abbot

Timothy & Sarah Abbot

Asa & Judith Abbot

Priscey Abbot

Charlotte, w. of Isaac Abbot

Wid. Dorcas Ames

Simeon & Sarah Ames

Wid. Experience Abbot

Wid. Lydia Abbot

Wid. Rebecca Abbot

Wid. Sarah Abbot

Wid. Hannah Abbot

Zebadiah & Sarah Abbot

Herman & Lydia Abbot

Abiel & Hannah Abbot

Hannah, wife of Stephen
    Abbot

Abigail Abbot

John & Elizabeth Adams

David & Mary Blunt

Hezekiah & Mary Ballard

Isaac & Lois Blunt

Amos & Elizabeth Blan-
chard

Hannah, wife of Thomas
Boynton

Symonds Baker

Joshua & Hepzibah Bailey

Sarah, w. of Eppes Baker

Lydia, w. of Luther Bailey

William Bailey

Wid. Lucy Bailey

Hannah, w. of Benj. Berry

2

Wid. Mary Burt
Timothy & Mary Ballard
Jedediah & Sarah Burt
Lydia, w. of John Barnard

Fanny Blanchard
Wid. Hannah Bailey
Hannah, wife of Daniel
Beverly

Wid. Hannah Chandler
Wid. Rebecca Chandler
Rebecca Chandler
Isaac & Abigail Chandler
Joshua Chandler, jun.
Sam'l & Elizabeth Cogswell
Samuel jun. & Sarah Cogs-
  well

Joseph & Mary Chandler
Mary, w. of Abiel Chandler
Elizabeth Chandler
Florah Chandler
Wid. Hannah Chandler
Dorcas, wife of Joshua
  Chandler
Simon Crosby, jun.

Sally Corey

Simon & Deborah Crosby

Abijah & Hannah Clarke

James & Phebe Chandler

Samuel & Sarah Clarke

Dan'l & Hannah Cummings

Betsy Cleaveland

Mercy, w. of James Davis

Philemon Dane

Palfrey & Abigail Downing

Hannah, w. of Amos Durant

Priscilla, wife of Moses
Dane

Madam Abigail French

Jacob Foster

Wid. Hannah Foster

Wid. Mary Foster

Abiel & Lydia Faulkner

Samuel Farrar

Anna Foster

Wid. Elizabeth Frye

William Foster

Lucy Foster

Lucy, w. of Theo's Frye

Enoch & Mary Frye

John & Ruth Flint

Persis, wife of Timo: Frye

Peter & Elizabeth French

Simeon & Rachel Furbush

Rachel Furbush

Hannah, w. of Amos Frye

Benj. & Hannah Goldsmith

Mary, w. of Thomas Gray

David & Rebecca Gray

William jun. & Elizabeth
Griffin

Jonathan & Servia Griffin

Jeremiah & Sarah Goldsmith

William & Mary Griffin

Hannah, wife of John
Goldsmith

Jonathan Gleason

Wid. Abigail Holt Hannah, w. of Isaac Holt
Jemima Holt Paul & Elizabeth Hunt
Ezekiel & Elizabeth Hardy Zebadiah & Sarah Holt
Lydia, w. of Abiel Holt Elizabeth, w. of Jno. Hardy
Peter & Hepzibah Holt Hannah Holt
Wid. Abigail Holt Cloe, w. of Wm. Hawley
Isaac jun. & Tabitha Holt Dane & Lydia Holt
Henry & Anna Holt Jabez Hayward
Cloe, wife of John Holt. Rebecca Holt
Sarah, w. of John Harding Sarah Herrick.
Wid. Phebe Holt

Ezra & Dorothy Ingalls

2*

Jacob Jones

Wid. Fanny Johnson

Benjamin Jenkins

Elizabeth Jones

Wid. Dorcas Jones

Mary Jones

Elizabeth, wife of Ebenezer
    Jones

Rebecca, wife of John
    Kneeland

Joshua Lovejoy

Isaac & Mary Lovejoy

Ruth, w. of Isaac Lovejoy

Wid. Hannah Lee

Wid. Deborah Lovejoy

Elizabeth, wife of Samuel

Wid. Dorothy Lovejoy

    Lummus

Thomas & Mehitabel Man- Wid. Martha Mooar
    ning   Lydia, wife of Isaac Mooar

Dea. Mark Newman

Samuel & Hannah Osgood Hannah Osgood
Aaron & Esther Osgood

Deac'n Daniel & Hannah Wid. Mary Phelps
    Poor   Dorcas, w. of Isaac Phelps
Dea. Abiel Pearson   Deborah, wife of Daniel
Joseph & Rebecca Phelps   Poor, jun.
Elizabeth Patten   Elizabeth Adams Pearson
Wid. Lois Phelps   Mary Pearson
Wid. Mary Phelps

John Russell
Uriah & Hannah Russell
Ruth Richards
Wid. of Eben'r Rand

Caleb & Abigail Richardson
David Rice
Dorothy, w. of Asa Riggs

Mary Holyoke Sperrey
Wid. Sarah Stevens
Wid. Silence Swift
Zebadiah & Sarah Shat-
tuck
Joseph & Phebe Shattuck

Hannah, wife of Isaac
Shattuck
Lucy, w. of Sam'l Shattuck
Susannah, wife of Peter
Shattuck

William & Hannah Tucker Abiel & Mary Upton
Wid. Hannah Trow   Sally Upton

Ezekiel Wardwell   Phebe, wife of Nathan
Damaris Wardwell   Wardwell
Ruth, w. of Simon Ward- Esther, w. of John Wood
  well   John & Sarah Wardwell
                 Lydia Wardwell

CPSIA information can be obtained
at www.ICGtesting.com
Printed in the USA
LVOW10s2334230717
542370LV00030B/1275/P